Railways of Hampshire

Anthony W. Burges

Ian Allan
PUBLISHING

First published 2006

ISBN (10) 0 7110 3164 9
ISBN (13) 978 0 7110 3164 7

Published by Ian Allan Publishing

an imprint of Ian Allan Publishing Ltd,
Hersham, Surrey KT12 4RG
Printed in England by Ian Allan Printing Ltd,
Hersham, Surrey KT12 4RG

Code: 0609/A3

Visit the Ian Allan Publishing website at
www.ianallanpublishing.com

**This book is dedicated to
Dr Edwin Course — railway
historian, friend and mentor at
Southampton University**

Front cover: Rebuilt 'Merchant Navy'
No 35011 *General Steam Navigation*
approaches New Milton with a
Weymouth–Waterloo express in August 1964.
Anthony Burges

Back cover (top): 'Lord Nelson' No 30856
Lord St. Vincent pauses at Southampton
Central with a Waterloo–Bournemouth
semi-fast in January 1961. *Anthony Burges*

Back cover (middle): 'Hampshire' diesel-
electric multiple-unit No 1124 stops at
Horsebridge on an Andover Junction–
Portsmouth & Southsea service in
August 1964. *Anthony Burges*

Back cover (bottom): Rebuilt 'West Country'
No 34021 *Dartmoor* enters Grateley station
with a down West of England train in August
1964. *Anthony Burges*

Previous page: Having taken over at
Brockenhurst, 'Schools' No 30907 *Dulwich*
heads a Lymington Pier–Waterloo train away
from Southampton Central in the summer
of 1960. *G. R. Siviour*

Right: No 3440 *City of Truro* approaches
Northam at the beginning of its long cross-
country trek to Didcot on 11 May 1957.
On the extreme right is the Northam spur,
connecting Southampton Central and
Terminus stations. Northam is now the
location of the maintenance depot for the
Siemens 'Desiro' EMUs operated by
South West Trains. *Anthony Burges*

CONTENTS

FOREWORD

Reviewing 50-year-old photographs and sifting through records of the Hampshire of another era brings back a flood of memories. As a one-time student at Southampton University I have enduring recollections of holiday jobs as goods porter at Bevois Valley Yard in Southampton and, in the summertime, crane-painting in Southampton Docks, where I accidentally anointed a 'USA' tank engine with a pot of red lead paint when it stopped underneath the crane I was working on. The result was a unique livery which not even the most committed modeller would wish to replicate.

At the other end of the scale were the sheer delights of visits to the rustic Meon Valley line, where genial Guard Charlie Arthur always welcomed me like an old friend. I remember too the ear-splitting thrill of roaring through the inky blackness of the tunnels between Privett and West Meon on a motorised trolley in the company of the permanent-way gang. Leisurely brake-van rides to Bishops Waltham, Longparish and Gosport added a *frisson* of excitement and

novelty. Hiking with friends along the abandoned routes from Alton to Basingstoke, from Longparish to Hurstbourne and from Christchurch to Ringwood were exploratory challenges, particularly hacking a path through almost impenetrable undergrowth and brambles beyond Longparish; at that time it seemed that landowners were less assertive as far as property rights were concerned.

Among locomotive memories was the utter joy of having the majesty of *City of Truro* to myself on the DNSR and to hear the melodious clank and throaty exhaust tones of passing 'Greyhounds' on the 'Sprat & Winkle' line, while I enjoyed a pint in the garden of the Seven Stars at Fullerton. Users of electric services may recall the unforgettable aroma of stale tobacco, dust-impregnated upholstery and ozone that characterised the '2-BIL' units on the Waterloo–Alton line. These were notorious for 'hunting' (rough ride), so the experience was seldom compatible with a hastily consumed breakfast. Lastly, regular walks on

summer Saturdays along the line between my home at New Milton and Hinton Admiral to observe a never-ending cavalcade of steam always produced surprises. It really is a very different world now!

Acknowledgements

Without the opportunities created by the lineside and brake-van permits kindly provided by British Railways (Southern Region) this record of a bygone era would have been impoverished. Special thanks are due to my old friend from university days, Gerald Siviour, for supplementing my photographs with some of his own, and to my wife, Mary, for her patience as I relived the past during the preparation of this book. Michael Bowie, of Lux Photographic Services, of Carleton Place, Ontario, performed miracles in breathing new life into my 50-year-old negatives.

Anthony Burges
Ottawa
June 2006

INTRODUCTION

The focus of this book is the 1950s, when steam traction was dominant and the rail network of Hampshire was 32% more extensive, in mileage terms, than that which exists today. As railways have historically evolved to serve the needs of the region, some reference to the transformation of the county during the period from 1950 to 2005 can provide a useful context in which to explain the sweeping changes that have occurred. Similarly, railway history as far back as the 1830s has left its mark, and this too deserves consideration.

Contemporary Hampshire reflects a type of transformation that is discernible throughout much of Britain. First and foremost, the county has become increasingly urbanised, and its population centres continue to grow. This trend is most obvious in the area bounded by Southampton, Portsmouth and Eastleigh. Market towns such as Basingstoke and Andover have been overwhelmed and reincarnated as industrial and business centres as a result of London-overspill housing policies. Equally profound changes are evident in rural areas, as commuters, retirees and weekenders seek to escape London. The availability of housing sites and the advent of easily accessible motorways,

plus an unprecedented level of car ownership, have combined to create serious traffic congestion. The urban infill and sprawl of coastal areas (with the exception of the New Forest) has produced a landscape that increasingly resembles the Sussex coastal plain. Greater affluence and low-cost air transport has diverted many holidaymakers to sunnier climes, and traditional resort areas from Bournemouth to Hayling Island have adapted to short-stay visitors and car-borne excursionists.

Southampton has consolidated its role as the major port and commercial centre of the South Coast. Global passenger-liner traffic has been lost to airline competition, and port facilities have been redeveloped to accommodate containerised freight technology, which is heavily (but not entirely) dependent on road transport. Elsewhere in the county competitive pressures and EU membership have resulted in an agricultural sector in which road haulage and agri-business go hand in hand, minimising the role of rail freight.

The long-established relationship between the county and the military has also changed. Although Salisbury Plain and the Aldershot area have retained some of their former strategic significance, the visibility of

Ministry of Defence activities has diminished, with many installations being closed, reduced in scale or converted for civilian use. Even the naval presence in the Portsmouth area is now a shadow of its former prominence.

These are but a few selected indicators that exemplify the contrast between the Hampshire of the 1950s and the prosperous — if more congested and polluted — environment that exists today. It is not surprising that the railway that has emerged from this period of change is vastly different in so many ways.

Such has been the transformation of Hampshire that not even the county boundaries have remained constant. So in order to avoid confusion and to facilitate comparisons between the railways of the 1950s and 2005, it is assumed that the reader will allow the author to take the liberty of ignoring the subsequent redrawing of county boundaries, of which the most notable was the transfer of the Bournemouth urban area to neighbouring Dorset. Throughout the book the reader may also note that the photographic pilgrimage has occasionally strayed across the county boundary, where adequate coverage of a specific line suggested it.

HAMPSHIRE'S RAILWAYS — AN OVERVIEW

An historical perspective

Three main lines form the principal components of the Hampshire rail network. The core is the route from London to Southampton, Bournemouth and Weymouth, crossing the county boundary near Farnborough in the north-east and Bournemouth in the south-west. An important offshoot — and a significant main line in itself — extends westward from Worting Junction, near Basingstoke, across the north of the county to Andover and Grateley before entering Wiltshire en route to Salisbury and Exeter. The eastern border of Hampshire from Liphook to Havant is roughly paralleled by a section of the Portsmouth direct line from Waterloo, electrified in 1937 and linking Woking and Guildford in Surrey to Portsmouth Harbour with its ferry connection for the Isle of Wight.

London & Southampton Railway

The London & Southampton Railway was one of the earliest trunk routes to be built in southern England and the first in Hampshire. It was opened for traffic from London (Nine Elms) to Shapley Heath (Winchfield) on 24 September 1838, followed by an extension to Basingstoke on 10 June 1839. South of Basingstoke this double-track line, with a ruling gradient of 1 in 250, struck out boldly in a southerly direction across chalk downland, passing through four tunnels before reaching Winchester. Further south construction proceeded rapidly, and a temporary terminus at Southampton (Northam Road) was linked to Winchester via the Itchen valley, for much of the way following the general route of the Itchen Navigation, on 10 June 1839.

Completion of the line between Basingstoke and Winchester ensured the opening of the entire line as originally conceived between Nine Elms and Southampton Town (later Terminus) on 11 May 1839. The project was part of an integrated development in which the expansion of the docks at Southampton was to play an essential role. (This would be reaffirmed in 1892 when the LSWR — successor to the London & Southampton Railway — purchased the greatly enlarged docks.) Famous personages of the pioneer days of the railway industry such as Joseph Locke (engineer), Thomas Brassey (contractor) and William Tite (architect) played key roles in the construction of the new main line. When train services began much of the country crossed by the London & Southampton was thinly populated, and

the only intermediate stations deemed necessary to serve the rural areas were those at Farnborough, Shapley Heath (now Winchfield), and Andover Road (now Micheldever).

Important offshoots to Fareham and Gosport in 1841 and to Romsey and Salisbury (Milford) in 1847 were instrumental in establishing the town of Bishopstoke (now Eastleigh) as an important junction on the new line. The opening of the rail link to Gosport prompted the company to change its name to the London & South Western Railway (LSWR) in deference to the complaints of citizens of the adjacent port and naval base of Portsmouth, which regarded Southampton as a competitor.

Southampton & Dorchester Railway

The arrival of the LSWR soon sparked interest in railway development to the west of Southampton, and Charles Castleman, a Wimborne solicitor, promoted the Southampton & Dorchester Railway. This company built a line from Southampton (Blechynden) across the New Forest to Brockenhurst and westward to Ringwood and beyond the county border to Wimborne, Wareham and Dorchester, which opened on 1 June 1847. (The ensuing inconvenience for passengers changing stations at Southampton was eventually resolved by the construction of the Northam curve, which linked the two lines in July 1858.) At the outset the market towns of Ringwood and Wimborne were perceived as offering better traffic prospects. As a result the new railway to Dorchester veered away from the sparsely populated coast, where Christchurch was the only significant community as Bournemouth was yet to develop. Thus, in taking this somewhat circuitous route, the new railway rapidly earned the sobriquet 'Castleman's Corkscrew'.

Initially the only intermediate stations in Hampshire were at Redbridge, Lyndhurst Road, Beaulieu Road (which was to have a chequered early existence, being closed from February 1860 until November 1895), Brockenhurst, Christchurch Road (later renamed Holmsley) and Ringwood. Christchurch was connected by a branch from Ringwood (closed in 1935). It was not until 5 March 1888 that a more direct route (now a part of the Bournemouth main line) was opened between Brockenhurst and Christchurch, with stations at Sway, New Milton and Hinton (later renamed Hinton Admiral after a nearby country seat); the old line, thereafter referred to as 'the old road', then assumed a secondary status, and a

connection was established at Christchurch with a link from Bournemouth that had been opened in 1870.

The legacy of this piecemeal evolutionary process became the busy main line of today. As late as 1958 the London–Southampton section was handling as many as 2,900 freight trains annually to and from Southampton Docks plus several hundred ocean liner expresses and a fairly intensive service of main-line and local passenger trains. In the 1950s pride of place was occupied by the all-Pullman 'Bournemouth Belle' (1931-67, with wartime interruptions) and the 'Royal Wessex' (1951-67). Inter-regional services to the Midlands and the North, which were mostly restricted to summer Saturdays, often placed heavy demands on the diminishing pool of motive power. On such occasions interesting photographic opportunities abounded: 'Castleman's Corkscrew' played a vital role as a diversionary route for peak-period trains serving Weymouth and Swanage, while the relative tranquillity of the Lymington Pier branch was disturbed by occasional through trains to/from Waterloo.

In the early 1950s the main line presented the intriguing spectacle of a busy steam trunk route on which operated a varied assortment of motive power, ranging from 19th-century veterans designed by Dugald Drummond to more recent Bulleid Pacifics and new BR standard types. Passenger and freight rolling stock was equally varied, and many pre-Grouping relics lingered for a few more years.

Further embellishments which added character to the line (and which are still fondly remembered) were the massive lineside advertisements that reminded the traveller that 'You are entering [or leaving] the Strong Country' (named after a now-vanished Romsey brewer). Such messages reinforced a sense of belonging when seen from the carriage window as the green and rolling swathe of Hampshire downland unfolded between Basingstoke and Winchester.

The main-line route west of Basingstoke — from Andover Junction to Salisbury and beyond — was built in response to pressure from the local community and the ever-present threat of encroachment by the GWR, which persuaded a somewhat reluctant LSWR to build a line to forestall intrusion into its territory by competitors. Blank spaces on the railway map were often regarded as invitations for encroachment, and the protection of territory and pre-emptive network expansion were recurring themes throughout the LSWR period. Thus at the time it was entirely logical for the LSWR to construct a line westwards to Andover in 1854 and on to Salisbury in 1857.

The new route pursued a direct course across the northern part of the county, where the chalk upland of Salisbury Plain presented no insurmountable obstacles to progress. In the early 1950s it was still competing with its old rival — the (G)WR main line from Paddington — for the flourishing seasonal holiday traffic to Devon and Cornwall. Military traffic to and from Salisbury Plain remained strong, and a network of feeder lines, from as far as the westernmost extremity of the 'Withered Arm', at Padstow, continued to contribute to a healthy, if seasonal, traffic flow. Named expresses such as the legendary 'Atlantic Coast Express' (1907-64), on which the author enjoyed

holiday trips to Ilfracombe and Bude, and the all-Pullman 'Devon Belle' (1947-54), with its renowned observation cars, confirmed its main-line status, although the route was not as busy as the Bournemouth line.

The future would not be so rosy. Inter-regional transfers of control, closure of smaller country stations, reduction in line capacity, the loss of most branch lines west of Salisbury, the end of steam traction and the truncation of services west of Exeter combined to reduce the LSWR's West of England main line to a shadow of its former glory. In the late 1950s the invasion of the diesel-electrics, which took over local services between Salisbury, Basingstoke and Reading, was the precursor of the growth of Andover and the expansion of commuting to London which partially offset the diminished role of this formerly strategic route.

Portsmouth Direct Railway

The Portsmouth Direct line crosses difficult terrain, which imposed a ruling gradient of 1 in 80, requiring much curvature and necessitated a tunnel through the South Downs at Buriton. Typically, the line was the LSWR's answer to the demands of Portsmouth, the pressures of other local interests, the threat of competition from the London, Brighton & South Coast Railway (LBSCR) and the brief prospect of regional intrusion by the South Eastern Railway (SER) resulted in the LSWR's assuming control.

Thus a new main line connecting London and Portsmouth via Woking, Guildford and Petersfield was opened for business on 1 January 1859. However, the LSWR did not afford the line any special status and the route was not destined to gain a fast and frequent service until it was electrified by the SR in 1937.

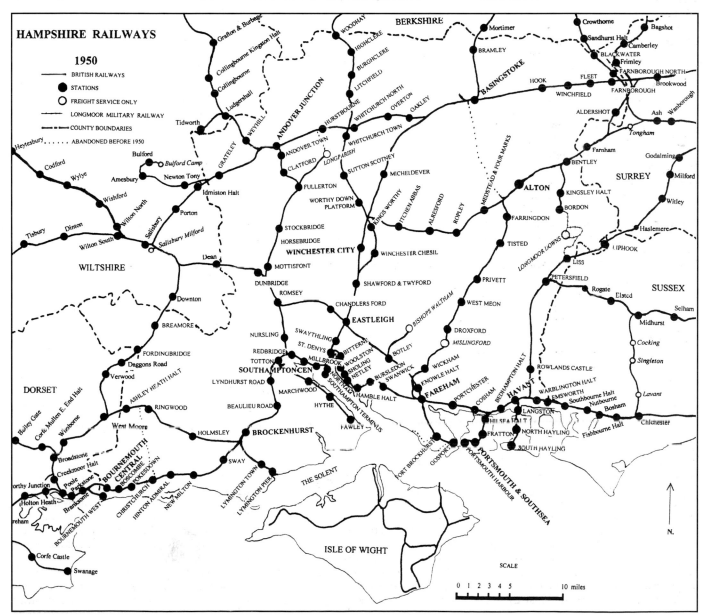

In the early days the LSWR's operations between Portsmouth and the junction with the LBSCR at Havant were occasionally impeded by a somewhat fraught relationship between the two companies. This was an echo of their earlier open conflict at the 'Battle of Havant', during a time when bare-knuckle competition was in vogue. Difficulties were resolved by a joint-operating agreement on Portsea Island. In the 1950s the Portsmouth Direct was the domain of a typical SR regular-interval electric service in which the faster schedules were maintained by the impressive '4-COR' units running in combinations of up to 12 coaches, while stopping trains usually consisted of two of the notoriously rough-riding '2-BIL' units. Apart from a well-established commuter business, there was still a healthy seasonal Isle of Wight holiday traffic. Today new Siemens electric units are much in evidence, the commuter traffic to London has grown, but the heavy traffic to the Isle of Wight, while remaining, is unlikely ever to regain its former importance. In spite of modern rolling stock the physical limitations of the route preclude much high-speed operation.

Defending the territory

The railway history of Hampshire has been characterised by the dominance of one company. Until the Grouping in 1923 the LSWR was the pre-eminent force. Other companies such as the GWR, LBSCR and SECR, in nibbling at the edges of the LSWR domain, exerted enough of a competitive threat to shape much of the ultimate network. Expansion of these rivals into Hampshire was largely thwarted by such devices as pre-emptive construction in hitherto untapped territory, strategic blocking of expansion, a non-aggression pact (with the GWR), and a joint operating agreement (with the LBSCR in the Portsmouth area). Basingstoke, Whitchurch, Andover, Winchester and Havant were locations where potential threats to the LSWR monopoly existed. Beyond the confines of the county, Salisbury and Guildford assumed similar strategic significance while the LSWR retaliated by threatening to extend its network to include Bristol to deflect a predatory GWR. Southampton was a particular target of the potential intruders. After 1923 the SR consolidated its stranglehold on Hampshire and the GWR presence was effectively confined to the northern periphery of the county at Basingstoke and Andover. The only exception was the GWR Newbury–Winchester line.

The latter, after a brief initial period of nominal corporate independence as the Didcot, Newbury & Southampton Railway (DNSR), was worked from its opening in 1891 as far as Winchester by the GWR. Originally conceived as a main line, it failed to gain independent access to Southampton and this was provided instead by the LSWR beyond Winchester Chesil (an example of defensive blocking strategy at work).

A proposed link from the DNSR at Whitchurch to the LSWR did not materialise. Instead the connection to Southampton and Bournemouth over LSWR metals via Hurstbourne and Fullerton was part of a pre-emptive strategy to ward off a perceived GWR expansion to tap the Bournemouth market. The outcome was the construction of one of Hampshire's more notable 'white elephant' railways, the Longparish line. Throughout its near 70 years of existence, the Newbury–Winchester route fulfilled the humble role of a purely local line running through a thinly populated area. Its north-south alignment ran counter to the east-west travel preferences of most of the on-line population. Although it achieved a fleeting strategic significance in World War 2, its value declined after 1945. Had it survived beyond 1964 it might have become a diversionary route for containerised freight with the development of Southampton as a major container port. Ironically, much of its route is now paralleled by a highway which groans under the impact of trucks carrying this traffic. By the 1950s the line had declined in importance and spent its remaining days as a charming but forgotten backwater that played temporary host to the resurrected *City of Truro* and as an occasional route for low-priority goods trains.

In contrast the GWR line from Reading to Basingstoke has always been of much greater significance for passenger and freight traffic. In the late 19th century the territory to the south of Basingstoke may have appeared, in strategic terms, to be an inviting space on the map offering a potential route to Portsmouth. Whether this concern was a factor in the decision of the LSWR to build the Basingstoke & Alton Light Railway (opened in 1901) and the Meon Valley line from Alton to Fareham (opened in 1903) is not verifiable and remains a matter for conjecture. In any event the LSWR laid claim to this railwayless void at considerable expense to itself and any potential advance by the GWR was averted. In the process two additional 'white elephants' were added to the Hampshire network.

The opening of the Swindon, Marlborough and Andover Junction Railway in 1882/3, subsequently the Midland & South Western Junction Railway (MSWJR), was the genesis of a new through route which connected with the Midland Railway at Cheltenham Spa. This was a development that served rather than conflicted with the interest of the LSWR. As a result of running rights agreements between the LSWR and MSWJR signed in 1892 and 1894, through goods and passenger services were inaugurated between Southampton and northern destinations such as Bradford, Leeds and Liverpool. In the 1923 Grouping the MSWJR was absorbed by the GWR, but by that date the danger of GWR encroachment was past. Weyhill was the only purely MSWJR station in Hampshire although the company maintained a separate shed at Andover Junction.

The route declined in the 1930s, but revived during World War 2 when it handled exceptionally heavy military traffic at the Hampshire/Wiltshire border stations of Ludgershall and Tidworth. The return of peace in 1945 saw a reversion to lower traffic levels, and service cutbacks in 1958 left only one surviving through train from Southampton to Cheltenham Spa and a vestigial local service. All that now remains of the MSWJR is the freight spur from Red Post Junction, Andover, to a military depot at Ludgershall and a short preserved section north of Swindon at Cricklade. The southern part of the through route from Andover Junction to Romsey was a double-track line through the sylvan valleys of the Anton and Test, where hourly but poorly patronised services continued until 1964.

Another strategic line which safeguarded the LSWR's leading position in Hampshire was the Salisbury & Dorset Junction line from Alderbury Junction (south of Salisbury) to West Moors in Dorset via the Avon valley and Fordingbridge built in 1866. The GWR had reached Salisbury from Warminster in 1856, nine years after the arrival of the LSWR from Bishopstoke. The West Moors line was used by through services to the GWR in earlier times but if public timetables are any indication, the line, which had Hampshire stations at Breamore and Fordingbridge, was never very busy and was probably marginal for much of its existence until closure in 1964. The author remembers it fondly as a bucolic happy hunting ground for 'Greyhounds' in the 1950s.

The examples provided suggest that the county was a chess board on which the LSWR sought to checkmate its opponents in defence of its territorial monopoly throughout the 19th century. It is interesting to note that only one of the lines mentioned survives today — a certain indication of the way the game has changed!

The old order changes with a vengeance

Rationalisation and restructuring are familiar euphemisms, often used to sweeten the pill of railway-line and station closures. In the second half of the 20th century Hampshire did not escape the axe that decimated so much of the national rail network. Today the landscape of the county is littered — and its industrial archæology enriched — with the fading remnants of lost railways.

Two important measures suggest, at first glance, a major contraction in the significance of rail. Firstly, the total national rail route mileage in Hampshire has declined from 322 in 1950 to 219 in 2005. Secondly, there has been a reduction in the number of stations open for passenger traffic from 110 to 64. Paradoxically, the closure of branch lines and stations has not been reflected in the overall numbers of passengers carried, or the frequency of train services on the surviving lines. On the contrary, the reverse is true. This is attributable to a continuing expansion and concentration of passenger traffic on the main lines and commuter routes. In addition the service improvements which followed electrification were important factors. It is reasonable to assert that the remaining network is now generally recognised as an essential asset, and this has been reflected by its continuing modernisation.

As far as goods traffic is concerned, the situation is different, but there are grounds for optimism. The photographs reveal an age when virtually all stations in the county handled wagon-load traffic carried by slow-moving and often unfitted freight trains, whose slow progress limited track capacity. Necessary appendages to this system included intermediate yards for marshalling trains and a large fleet of locomotives dedicated to shunting and freight haulage. Southampton Docks was a pivotal point in the system. In addition there were bulk flows such as oil from the Esso refinery at Fawley, which remains a significant generator of traffic to this day. Multiple wagon-loads of military supplies were also important. A fundamental component of rail freight in the 1950s was the local distribution of household coal — a commodity that was destined to vanish by the end of the 20th century as a result of revolutionary changes in the energy sector. Other transport options would gradually deprive the railways of the once important mail and parcels traffic.

Towards a leaner and meaner railway
The first real sign of the changes that were to come was apparent in the autumn of 1957 with the replacement of most steam-hauled local services on the Portsmouth–Salisbury, Portsmouth–Andover Junction and Alton–Winchester services by diesel-electric multiple-units. This was followed by the Reading–Portsmouth service and local trains between Reading, Basingstoke and Salisbury. Main-line steam disappeared in 1967 with the electrification of the London (Waterloo)–Bournemouth and Brockenhurst–Lymington Pier routes. In fact the Bournemouth main line was to witness one of the last flourishes of steam traction on the Southern Region. All Basingstoke–Salisbury–Exeter services were dieselised in July 1967. The third rail was subsequently energised from Bournemouth to Weymouth in 1988 and from Havant/Hilsea to Southampton and Eastleigh via Fareham in 1990. Thus by 2005 68% of the rail network in Hampshire was electrified, and all but 10 of the remaining passenger stations were located on electrified lines.

Hampshire endured its fair share of line closures during the second half of the 20th century. In the years preceding the release of the Beeching Report in 1963 a number of passenger services in Hampshire — and on the Ludgershall–Tidworth branch, on the Hampshire/Wiltshire border — were withdrawn. The 1950s saw the beginning of what became a somewhat melancholy period for railway enthusiasts, when attendance at frequent 'funerals' throughout Britain made heavy demands on time and resources as they attempted to witness and record as much as possible of a rapidly vanishing railway heritage. Concurrently, the deteriorating condition of the remaining fleet of steam locomotives did not inspire confidence.

The Beeching Report identified an additional five lines and a total of 20 Hampshire stations for closure. It also recommended the withdrawal of local services between Portsmouth, Netley, Southampton and Romsey, although these suggestions were not implemented. In addition to the lines listed, Beeching also suggested the closure of the following stations: Grateley, Hurstbourne, Oakley, Overton and Whitchurch North. Of this group only Hurstbourne (6 April 1964) and Oakley (17 April 1963) were closed. An earlier station closure was Nursling, on 16 September 1957.

Other sections to have vanished from the railway map include freight connections that carried occasional special passenger traffic such as the Park Prewett Hospital spur at Basingstoke (1.0 miles) in 1954, the Royal Victoria Hospital spur at Netley (0.5 miles) in 1955 and Butts Junction (Alton)–Treloar Home (0.5 miles) in 1967.

The extensive Longmoor Military Railway linking Liss and Bordon ceased operation in 1978, while the MoD system at Bramley succumbed in 1987, leaving Marchwood as the county's sole surviving military railway. In addition the spurs serving the Royal Aircraft Establishment at Farnborough, the Admiralty Armaments Depot at Dean Hill, the US Army supply depot at Lockerly, the Thornycroft plant at Basingstoke and the Eling Tramway at Totton are now history.

Locomotive sheds were another feature of the railway scene that rapidly became redundant as a result of branch-line closures and the end of steam traction.

Hampshire has also witnessed the decline of railway workshops that traditionally were major employers of a multi-skilled workforce. When the London & South Western Railway (LSWR) moved its carriage and locomotive workshops from Nine Elms, in 1890 and 1909 respectively, the original choice was between greenfield sites at Andover or Eastleigh. The selection of Eastleigh resulted in the creation of one of Britain's major railway towns. In the ensuing years more than 400 locomotives were either built or reconstructed there, while the routine maintenance of steam power, diesel-electric multiple-units and a vast range of passenger and goods rolling stock was the backbone of the local economy.

All this was, however, destined to change. The fundamental restructuring of the rail sector and the franchising of train operations resulted in the transfer of Eastleigh Works to the private sector. This turned out to be an interim step, as foreign-based manufacturers rapidly began to supply much of the UK rail-equipment market. By the end of 2005 the hitherto unthinkable was about to happen, and the end of Eastleigh Works was nigh. Closure was announced, and plans were approved for the demolition of the sprawling workshop complex and the redevelopment of the site for non-railway use. This had been preceded by the closure of the former SR sleeper depot at Redbridge in the early 1990s and the absorption of the site to form part of the Dibden port redevelopment. The severing of old traditions that these changes imply symbolises the diminished role of the railway as a major generator of employment.

Summary of route mileage and stations in Hampshire 1850-2005							
	1850	1875	1900	1925	1950	1975	2005
Total route mileage	134.0	256.4	307.6	381.3	322.0	216.2	219.0
Electrified mileage					37.7	120.5	151.7
Stations open	29	75*	107*	142*	121*	71*	67**

* includes stations with restricted public access
** includes 16 unstaffed stations and three Mid-Hants Railway stations

Hampshire branch-line closures 1900-2005

	closure date	mileage	closed to	notes
Fratton–Southsea	August 1914	1.25	all traffic	
Forton Junction (Gosport)–Stokes Bay	1 November 1915	1.75	all traffic	
Basingstoke–Alton (Butts Junction)	1 January 1917	13	all traffic	1
Hurstbourne Junction–Longparish	6 July 1931	3.75	all traffic	
Longparish–Fullerton Junction	6 July 1931	3.25	passenger traffic only	
Fort Brockhurst–Lee on Solent	1 January 1931	3	passenger traffic only	
Basingstoke–Alton (Butts Junction)	12 September 1932	13	passenger traffic only	
Botley–Bishops Waltham	2 January 1933	3.75	passenger traffic only	
Ringwood–Christchurch	30 September 1935	6.7	all traffic	
Fort Brockhurst–Lee on Solent	30 September 1935	3	all traffic	
Basingstoke (Thornycroft Works)–Alton (Treloar Home)	1 June 1936	12.25	all traffic	2
Fareham–Gosport	8 June 1953	5	passenger traffic only	
Alton (Butts Junction)–Fareham	7 February 1955	23.25	passenger traffic only	
Farringdon–Droxford	7 February 1955	13	all traffic	
Petersfield–Midhurst (Sussex)	7 February 1955	2.25 †	all traffic	
Fullerton–Longparish	28 May 1955	3.25	all traffic	
Bentley–Bordon	16 September 1957	4.75	passenger traffic only	
Woodhay (Berks)–Shawford Junction	7 March 1960	35.25	passenger traffic only	
Red Post Junction (Andover)–Ludgershall (Wilts)	11 September 1961	5	passenger traffic only	
Havant–Hayling Island	4 November 1963	4.5	all traffic	
Fareham–Knowle (deviation)	6 April 1964	1.5	all traffic	
Brockenhurst (Lymington Junction)–West Moors (Dorset)	4 May 1964	13.75 †	all traffic	3*
Downton (Wilts)–Daggons Road (Dorset)	4 May 1964	4.75 †	all traffic	*
Woodhay (Berks)–Shawford Junction	9 August 1964	35.25 †	all traffic	
Romsey (Kimbridge Junction)–Andover Town	7 September 1964	14.25	all traffic	
Andover Junction–Andover Town	7 September 1964	0.75	passenger traffic only	
Bentley–Bordon	4 April 1966	4.75	all traffic	
Andover Junction–Andover Town	18 September 1967	0.75	all traffic	
Alton (Butts Junction)–Farringdon	13 August 1968	3.5	all traffic	
Knowle Junction–Droxford	13 August 1968	7	all traffic	
Fareham–Gosport	30 January 1969	5	all traffic	
Eastleigh–Romsey	5 May 1969	7.25	passenger traffic only	4
Alton–Winchester Junction	5 February 1973	16.75	all traffic	5*

1: temporary closure from 1 January 1917 to 18 August 1924
2: Alton–Treloar/Basingstoke–Thornycroft Works remained open for freight after 1936
3: Ringwood–West Moors remained open for freight until 1967
4: reopened for passengers 19 October 2003
5: subsequently partially reopened by Mid-Hants Railway
* Beeching recommendation
† mileage within Hampshire

Total mileages

	all traffic	passenger traffic only	notes
1900-1950	41.7 miles	22.5 miles	
1950-2000	115.5 miles	96 miles	6

6: Excludes Alton–Alresford (reopened by Mid-Hants Railway for passengers — Alresford–Ropley 30 April 1977 and Ropley–Alton 28 May 1983) and Eastleigh–Romsey (reopened for passengers 19 October 2003)

Improved prospects

The electrification of the Bournemouth line heralded the closure of Northam and Southampton Terminus stations on 5 September 1966, when all passenger services were concentrated at Southampton Central. In the south-west of the county, Boscombe was another casualty, due to its close proximity to Bournemouth Central and Pokesdown, while the terminus at Bournemouth West was also closed and demolished. Part of the short branch line on which it stood provided a site for the construction of new sheds for the incoming EMUs. These Bournemouth-area changes occurred in September/October 1965. A positive step was the linking of Southampton Airport to the rail network with the opening of a new if somewhat utilitarian station named Southampton Airport Parkway in April 1965.

Since the 1970s there have been further signs of a revival in the fortunes of Hampshire's railways. Modernisation has brought about the gradual replacement (as far as the Bournemouth electrification is concerned) of its fleet of first-generation slam-door multiple-units, so that the only slam-door trains remaining in Hampshire are the so-called 'vintage' units allocated to the Lymington Pier branch. The reliable but unglamorous 'Hampshire' DEMUs were finally withdrawn or transferred elsewhere in 1998, replaced by second- and third-generation DMUs.

Another notable development was the reopening to passengers in 2003 of the Eastleigh-Romsey line and the construction of a new station at Chandlers Ford, served by a local service from Southampton. Housing developments at Hedge End, between Eastleigh and Botley, resulted in the opening of a new station in 1992. These were small steps, perhaps, but are indications of a growing awareness of the role that railways must play in the rapid urban expansion that is taking place around Southampton.

Hampshire locoshed closures 1950-67

	code	closure date
Bordon	–	1951
Gosport	71D*	1953
Winchester Chesil (GW)	82C* (71A* from 1952)	1953
Andover Junction (GW)	82C* (71A* from 1952)	1958
Fratton	71D (70F from 1956)	1959
Andover Junction (SR)	71A*	1962
Lymington	71A* (70D* from 1963)	1967
Southampton Docks	71I (70I from 1963)	1966
Basingstoke	70D (70D* from 1963)	1967
Bournemouth	71B (70F from 1963)	1967
Eastleigh	71A (70D from 1963)	1967
Winchester City (SR)	71A* (70D* from 1963)	1969 (closed to steam in 1963)

* denotes sub-shed

Notwithstanding the loss of cross-country routes to Newbury and Didcot and to Swindon and Cheltenham Spa, there has been an improvement in cross-country links from Bournemouth and Southampton to the Midlands and the North via Reading with regular-interval fast trains. Portsmouth and Southampton continue to be connected to Bristol and Cardiff by popular regular services.

A further cause for optimism has been the successful restoration of steam-hauled passenger trains from Alton to Alresford by the Mid-Hants Railway. Back in the 1950s few would have predicted that Ropley would become the site of the last remaining facility in the county capable of undertaking a wide range of maintenance services for steam locomotives.

Above: Rebuilding of 'West Country' No 34045 *Ottery St. Mary* in progress at Eastleigh Works in September 1958. *Anthony Burges*

Left: A Bournemouth–Waterloo semi-fast headed by '4-REP' No 3008 stops briefly at the bare platforms of Southampton Airport Parkway on 2 September 1971. *Anthony Burges*

Right: Seen in June 1971, the former stationmaster's house and principal station building (which housed a post office) dating from 1840, a stark restored island platform adorned only with the inevitable bus shelter and a simplified track layout were components of the changed scene at Micheldever following electrification. Notwithstanding the apparent downgrading, this rural station now handles unprecedented numbers of London commuters. The prospect of major housing development in the area is likely to further transform its role and appearance. *Anthony Burges*

BOURNEMOUTH MAIN LINE

Left: An interesting contrast at Basingstoke was provided on 18 March 1957 by 'Merchant Navy' No 35030 *Elder-Dempster Lines* on a down West of England train and prototype 'Hastings' diesel-electric multiple-unit No 1001, which had arrived after a test run from Eastleigh, on which speeds of around 100mph had been attained near Micheldever. *Anthony Burges*

Left: 'U'-class Mogul No 31800 stops at Micheldever on 19 May 1956 with a down stopping train composed exclusively of ex-LSWR non-corridor stock in green livery. By the 1950s the island platform had been out of use for many years. Subsequent electrification and resignalling resulted in the removal of the signal cabin, the reincarnation of the island platform and the loss of the outer slow lines, although, perhaps surprisingly, the principal station building was retained. Micheldever was a pleasant spot from which to observe traffic on an all-steam main line. Its extensive sidings also housed many withdrawn first-generation SR electric multiple-units and pre-Grouping carriages awaiting disposal at Eastleigh. Nearby, buried deep in the chalk, were large oil-storage facilities, served by occasional trainloads of tanker wagons. *Anthony Burges*

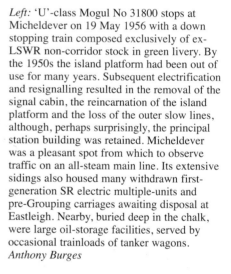

Left: On 20 July 1959, some eight years before electrification and when locomotives were often smartly turned out, unrebuilt 'West Country' No 34008 *Padstow* is about to leave Winchester City with a Waterloo–Bournemouth train. *Anthony Burges*

Right: 'West Country' No 34010 *Sidmouth* shakes Shawford & Twyford station to its foundations as it hurtles through with a down Bournemouth express, also on 5 June 1957. *Anthony Burges*

Right: Between Winchester and Eastleigh, in the valley of the Itchen, lies the small country station of Shawford & Twyford (now Shawford). It has always been ignored by main-line expresses, although in the 1950s its service of stopping trains was supplemented by workings to the mid-Hants line to Alton and the ex-GW line to Newbury and Didcot. Typical of the local service on 5 June 1957 was this southbound three-coach train hauled by 'S15' 4-6-0 No 30515, designed by Urie for freight traffic. Built in 1921, it would be withdrawn in 1963. *Anthony Burges*

Below: Collett '2251' 0-6-0 No 2240 ambles into Shawford & Twyford with a Southampton Terminus–Newbury train on 5 June 1957, at which time the small goods yard was still dealing with a declining volume of wagon-load traffic. In the background can be seen the Shawford-avoiding line. *Anthony Burges*

Left: Against the backdrop of Eastleigh Works on 2 June 1953, 'Hall' 4-6-0 No 4919 *Donnington Hall* prepares to leave Eastleigh with a Reading General–Portsmouth & Southsea train. *Anthony Burges*

Below: It's 17 January 1957, and the first diesel-electric multiple-unit to be built to conform to the restricted loading gauge of the tunnels on the Tunbridge Wells Central–Hastings line has emerged from Eastleigh Works a few hours earlier. Here unit No 1001 has arrived at Eastleigh after its first test run to Botley and back. Once this initial order was completed the diesel revolution in Hampshire would begin, with the initial delivery of 22 two-car units that would gradually take over operation of Portsmouth–Southampton–Salisbury, Portsmouth–Eastleigh–Andover Junction and Southampton Central–Alton services. *Anthony Burges*

Left: Eastleigh shed contained a fine array of Southern power on Coronation Day, 2 June 1953, and the legendary hole in the fence was particularly busy on that occasion. Heading the line-up was Urie 'H15' No 30477 (built 1924, withdrawn 1959), in the company of veteran Drummond 'D15' No 30464 4-4-0 (built 1912, scrapped 1954), 'Merchant Navy' Pacific No 35022 *Holland America Line* (rebuilt 1956), and 'Z'-class 0-8-0T No 30952 (one of the last heavy shunting locomotives built by the Southern, in 1929). *Anthony Burges*

Right: Urie 'H15' No 30524 threads its way through the back gardens of Southampton after a stop at St Denys as it trundles along with an Eastleigh–Bournemouth West stopping train in October 1957. *Anthony Burges*

Right: Southampton Terminus dated from the opening of the London & Southampton Railway in 1840. By the mid-1950s its dockland location was no longer convenient for access to the city, which had long since expanded to the west. For operating purposes the station was a useful starting point for a limited number of slow trains that served Portsmouth & Southsea, Eastleigh, Alton, Bournemouth, and Andover Junction, but the Central station was by now long-established as the city's principal passenger station. Terminus station would be closed on 5 September 1966 as part of the revision of train services and the resignalling preceding electrification of the Bournemouth main line, its platforms subsequently being removed, but its impressive main building, designed by Sir William Tite and seen here on 11 May 1957, survives as a casino. *Anthony Burges*

Right: The proximity of Southampton Terminus to the docks is evident from this scene recalling the last years of Southampton as a liner port with worldwide connections. Boat expresses from London did not use the Terminus station, the now-demolished Ocean Liner Terminal having been built specifically for that purpose. On 11 May 1957 *City of Truro* graces the station with its august presence before returning to Didcot. Looming above is the former South Western Hotel, which building had reverted to office use after being taken over by the Royal Navy during World War 2. In 2001 it was converted to apartments. *Anthony Burges*

Left: In the 1950s Southampton Terminus was 'Greyhound' territory. In this view, recorded on 11 May 1957, No 30702 has been assigned to an all-stations to Portsmouth & Southsea turn, while No 30730 is awaiting its next duty. Visible beyond is the avoiding line giving access to the docks. The large number of wagons that are entering the docks have long since been supplanted by container trains. *Anthony Burges*

Above: This 'USA' 0-6-0T, built by the Vulcan Ironworks in the United States in 1942, was located by Oliver Bulleid, Chief Mechanical Engineer of the SR, in a dump of US Army war-surplus equipment at Newbury Racecourse in 1945. It and 12 other Vulcans, plus one built by Porter, were familiar features at Southampton Docks from 1946 to 1967, performing shunting work. Seen in 1960, No 30064 is moving empty boat-train stock to the New Docks. This locomotive is now preserved on the Bluebell Railway. *G. R. Siviour*

Left: 'D15' No 30464 would not have been unduly taxed by a four-coach stopping train for Andover Junction, seen at Southampton Central on 2 June 1953. Capable engines, the 'D15s' were occasionally assigned to Summer Saturday through trains from Waterloo to Lymington Pier. *Anthony Burges*

Above: Looking quite resplendent after emerging from rebuilding at Eastleigh Works, 'Merchant Navy' No 35020 *Bibby Line* is seen at Lyndhurst Road on a running-in turn with an Eastleigh–Bournemouth West slow train on 5 May 1956. *Anthony Burges*

Right: Scarcely disturbing the tranquillity of the New Forest, Standard Class 4 No 76014 drifts quietly away from Beaulieu Road on 5 May 1956 with a stopping train for Eastleigh. *Anthony Burges*

Right: Situated in the depths of the New Forest and three miles from the village famous for its motor museum and stately home, Beaulieu Road was (and continues to be) one of the least-used stations on the Bournemouth line. Among the few trains to stop there was this slow train for Eastleigh, hauled on 5 May 1956 by Standard Class 4 No 76014. The busiest day of the year at this isolated station was that of the Annual New Forest pony round-up and sale. *Anthony Burges*

Left: The junction at Brockenhurst was particularly busy on summer Saturdays, when main-line services between London, Bournemouth, Swanage and Weymouth were significantly augmented. In addition there were inter-regional holiday services such as this train for Bradford on 30 June 1956 hauled by 'King Arthur' 4-6-0 No 30739 *Sir Balan*. *Anthony Burges*

Left: The branch lines from Brockenhurst were busier on summer Saturdays too. The loop line to Bournemouth via Wimborne, known variously as 'Castleman's Corkscrew' or 'the old road', was used also by seasonal holiday services linking Waterloo to Swanage and Weymouth. In addition to these workings were the local branch trains, which remained in the hands of the faithful Drummond 'M7' tanks. Here on 30 June 1956 No 30104 prepares to take water before propelling its auto-train to Bournemouth West. *Anthony Burges*

Below: Summer Saturday through services from Waterloo to Lymington Pier brought unusual power such as 'Schools' and 'D15s' to Brockenhurst, while 'Qs' and 'Q1s' performed on the branch line. Here, on 30 June 1956, a 'Q1' 'Austerity' 0-6-0 —a type not normally seen on passenger duties —has received the right-away for Lymington Pier. *Anthony Burges*

Above: Sway has always been a relatively quiet village station served mainly by local trains, although the heavier consists of semi fast trains on the London–Bournemouth service would occasionally require the entire length of its platforms. 'Lord Nelsons' were typical of these workings; seen here on an up train on 30 June 1956 is No 30851 *Sir Francis Drake. Anthony Burges*

Right: An unusual local service stopping at Sway on 30 June 1956 was this Eastleigh–Wimborne train comprising five LSWR non-corridor coaches hauled by 'T9' No 30117. All available power was pressed into service on Saturdays. *Anthony Burges*

Left: 'Schools' 4-4-0s were not regularly employed on the Bournemouth line. No 30926 *Repton*, a locomotive with an unexpected future ahead of it, makes rapid progress through New Milton with a down train on 18 July 1959. *Anthony Burges*

Below: Veteran 'T9s' were still at work on the Eastleigh–Wimborne slow train in 1959, when grimy No 30120 was photographed making a dignified exit from New Milton. *Anthony Burges*

Bottom: Less-than-pristine 'West Country' No 34041 *Wilton* has time in hand on a lightweight up stopping train on 18 July 1959 at the unspoilt LSWR station of Hinton Admiral. *Anthony Burges*

Right: The busy interior of the trainshed at Bournemouth Central on 14 June 1959, when the centre roads were in frequent use by locomotives detaching stock from main-line trains. The advent of electrification in 1967 removed the need for these additional tracks and resulted in much simplification of the layout. *Anthony Burges*

Right: The all-Pullman 'Bournemouth Belle' was the pride of the line. On 14 June 1959 rebuilt 'Merchant Navy' Pacific No 35021 *New Zealand Line* looks immaculate as it awaits the green flag for London. *Anthony Burges*

Below: Rebuilt 'Merchant Navy' No 35022 *Holland America Line* leaves Bournemouth Central on 14 July 1959 with a train from Waterloo to Weymouth. Note the auto-train from Brockenhurst via Wimborne, which has just arrived. The structure on the left is Bournemouth loco shed. *Anthony Burges*

BASINGSTOKE–SALISBURY

Above: In the summer of 1962 Urie 'S15' No 30514 passes the quiet country station of Oakley with a long westbound goods train. Oakley was to be one of many casualties amongst Hampshire's minor stations, closing on 17 June 1967. *G. R. Siviour*

Left: This view of Hurstbourne station, situated some distance from the villages of Hurstbourne Priors and St Mary Bourne, is dated 1 June 1957. Prior to the opening of the station and the Longparish branch on 1 December 1882 there was a siding here, serving the nearby Hurstbourne Park Estate. In a rural setting to the east of the prominent brick Hurstbourne Viaduct, which carried the main line to Salisbury and the West across the valley of the River Bourne, the station was a loading point for the produce of the nearby watercress beds, which was consigned by passenger train to London markets. This traffic survived in the mid-1950s, and closure of the station would not occur until 6 May 1963 to passenger services; part of the site would subsequently be taken over by a scrap merchant. A flight of stairs connected the attractive station building to the wooden platform on an embankment. *Anthony Burges*

Above: Hurstbourne differed from other stations on the Basingstoke–Salisbury section in having wooden platforms and shelters. Passengers were something of a rarity, and on 1 June 1957 'West Country' No 34010 *Sidmouth* was, like most trains, passing at speed, with an up Waterloo express. Note the roof of the goods shed, visible on the right. *Anthony Burges*

Below: A most unusual visitor to Grateley on 14 May 1955 was Beattie 2-4-0WT No 30587, returning to Andover Junction with a railtour special from Bulford Camp. Grateley was later reduced to a 'basic station' with minimal facilities. *Anthony Burges*

Left: The stark platforms of Idmiston Halt, photographed on 1 June 1957, nestled in the chalk upland of Salisbury Plain where the military influence was dominant. The halt, situated across the Wiltshire border, was constructed in response to the needs of local army training facilities and existed from 3 January 1943 until closure on 9 September 1968. There was at one time a weekday workmen's train service to/from Salisbury. *Anthony Burges*

Centre left: 'Merchant Navy' No 35004 *Cunard White Star Line* seems to be excessive power for a Waterloo–Salisbury stopping train, seen on 1 June 1957 at Idmiston Halt, although such apparent anomalies were not uncommon in the period before the decline of steam power. *Anthony Burges*

Bottom left: A view recorded on 1 June 1957, looking west from the footbridge at Porton station. Like Idmiston Halt, to the east, Porton station would close on 9 September 1968, leaving Grateley as the only intermediate station between Andover and Salisbury. *Anthony Burges*

Above right: The wayside station of Porton evoked visions of unspeakable activities at the nearby Chemical & Biological Warfare Establishment at Porton Down. Passenger services here were somewhat sparse, and army personnel tended to prefer the frequent service provided by the graffiti-prone buses of Silver Star Motor Services to reach Salisbury and its faster trains to London. A more leisurely alternative was a stopping train such as that hauled on 1 June 1957 by 'S15' No 30828. The gantry crane which dominates the yard was formerly a transfer facility for the 60cm-gauge Porton Down Military Railway. *Anthony Burges*

Right: Principal trains on the West of England main line in 1957 dwarfed those of today in terms of length and seating capacity. Having taken over this heavy train at Salisbury, 'Merchant Navy' Pacific No 35004 *Cunard White Star Line* is still accelerating as it passes Porton on 1 June. *Anthony Burges*

BROCKENHURST–WIMBORNE

Above: The 'Castleman's Corkscrew' really came to life on summer Saturdays, when certain Weymouth and Swanage trains avoided congestion in the Bournemouth area and were diverted via Ringwood. On 30 June 1956 'West Country' No 34095 *Brentor* passes Holmsley at speed with a Weymouth–Waterloo train. Main-line expresses routed via Ringwood did not stop at intermediate stations on 'the old road'. *Anthony Burges*

Below: Peace and quiet at the New Forest wayside station of Holmsley are hardly disturbed by the arrival on 30 June 1956 of a Brockenhurst– Bournemouth West auto-train hauled by Drummond 'M7' tank No 30057. Note that goods traffic was still being handled, the crane showing signs of recent use. *Anthony Burges*

Right: 'M7s' and LSWR non-corridor auto-sets were the norm on many Hampshire branch-line services. In this classic scene No 30104 exemplifies the relaxed atmosphere of the Ringwood loop as its train for Brockenhurst awaits non-existent passengers at Holmsley on 30 June 1956. *Anthony Burges*

Right: Well-maintained double track stretching eastwards to the main line at Lymington Junction is evidence of the important diversionary role of the Ringwood loop as a relief line. Holmsley had, however, lost its importance of a century before, when it was known as Christchurch Road. Note that the length of the platforms far exceeded the requirements of stopping trains in the mid-1950s and that a footbridge was deemed unnecessary. The date is 30 June 1956. *Anthony Burges*

Right: Following closure of the loop line in 1964 road replaced rail at Holmsley, and the peace of the steam era was shattered forever. The notice announces the sale at auction of the station building, which would subsequently be enlarged and is now a tea room. *Anthony Burges*

Left: 'M7' No 30058 propels a Bournemouth West–Brockenhurst train at Ringwood on 3 May 1958. The abundant cycle racks were probably used by students commuting to Brockenhurst Grammar School. *Anthony Burges*

Centre: Ringwood station from the east on 3 May 1958. Note the bay platform, used until 1935 by trains on the Christchurch (via Hurn) line; also the typical LSWR signalbox, cattle pens and goods shed. The site has since been redeveloped. *Anthony Burges*

Bottom left: On 3 May 1958 a Brockenhurst auto-train powered by 'M7' No 30058 approaches Ringwood after crossing the water meadows of the River Avon. The site of the junction with the former branch to Christchurch lay about one mile to the west. Parts of this section to Ashley Heath have now been incorporated into the Castleman Trailway. *Anthony Burges*

Above right: Ashley Heath Halt, seen here on 3 May 1958, was a later addition, having been opened on 1 April 1927. It was a typical product of the SR pre-cast-concrete plant at Exmouth Junction. Beyond the level crossing the line skirted the Ringwood Forest before crossing the Avon Valley. *Anthony Burges*

Right: It's 19 August 1955, and just across the border in Dorset 'M7' No 30111 powers a Brockenhurst–Bournemouth West train at West Moors. East of the station is the junction with the line to Salisbury via Fordingbridge, beyond which are sidings laid by the War Department in 1943. Road and housing developments have now obliterated much of the trackbed in this area. *Anthony Burges*

BROCKENHURST–LYMINGTON PIER BRANCH

Above: The Brockenhurst–Lymington Pier line now has the distinction of being the only surviving branch with passenger service (with the exception of the Mid-Hants Railway's preserved line) in the county. In steam days the architecturally striking station at Lymington Town occupied a compact site replete with trainshed (now removed), bookstall, a small shed for the branch locomotive and goods facilities. Both of the latter no longer exist. In the 1950s vintage enamel advertisements (now highly collectable) adorned the station building. Notwithstanding these changes the station has continued to benefit from its central location in the town and generates a healthy level of passenger traffic, now conveyed in 'vintage' slam-door electric multiple-units. *Anthony Burges*

Left: On summer Saturdays holidaymakers *en route* to the scenic western end of the Isle of Wight could avail themselves of a through service to and from London. On 30 June 1956 a return train from Lymington Pier to Waterloo enters Lymington Town hauled by an 'M7' which will hand over to main-line power such as a 'Schools' 4-4-0 at Brockenhurst. Only half of the eight-coach train could be accommodated at the short platform. *Anthony Burges*

Above: In June 1956 a 'Q' 0-6-0 eases a Waterloo–Lymington Pier through train along the embankment from the town station to the ferry terminal on an inlet of the Solent. The 'Q' had taken over this relatively heavy train at Brockenhurst for the final branch-line portion of the journey. *Anthony Burges*

Below: Facilities at Lymington Pier station were more impressive in the 1950s, with extensive shelter for passengers, an additional track for locomotive release and a signalbox. Here the Yarmouth car ferry awaits the arrival of the connecting rail service. The scene contrasts with today's 'basic railway', with its more exposed platform, bus shelter, extensive car park and 'vintage' three-coach electric units. *Anthony Burges*

TOTTON–FAWLEY BRANCH

Above: 'M7' No 30375 leaves Marchwood with a rake of LSWR stock forming a Fawley–Southampton Central train on 5 May 1956. Although the Fawley branch was one of the newest lines in Hampshire, dating from 1925, its passenger trains had a decidedly pre-Grouping flavour in the 1950s.
Anthony Burges

Left: On 30 June 1956 we see 'M7' No 30378 with a Fawley–Southampton train near Pooks Green crossing, between Marchwood and Totton. The vestigial passenger services on the branch were designed to meet the needs of workers at the Esso oil refinery at Fawley.
Anthony Burges

EASTLEIGH–FAREHAM

Above: A brisk winter's morning near Boorley Green presented interesting contrasts in motive power. In the first of two photographs an 'M7' raises the echoes with a well-loaded return goods from Bishops Waltham to Eastleigh on 17 January 1957. *Anthony Burges*

Below: Minutes later the countryside near Boorley Green was disturbed by the ear-shattering roar and accompanying whine emitted by brand-new 'Hastings' diesel-electric multiple-unit No 1001 on one of a series of test runs from Eastleigh Works. Unacceptable decibel levels necessitated early modifications to protect the eardrums of passengers. *Anthony Burges*

Left: 'West Country' No 34011 *Tavistock* speeds through Botley with a Portsmouth & Southsea–Birmingham Snow Hill train on 2 June 1956. The Bishops Waltham branch is visible on the far left. *Anthony Burges*

Right: 'U'-class Mogul No 31637 leaves Botley on 2 June 1956 with a lightweight train of LSWR non-corridor stock *en route* from Portsmouth & Southsea to Salisbury. *Anthony Burges*

Left: Botley was the junction for the freight-only Bishops Waltham branch. The bay platform used by branch trains in the days of passenger service (withdrawn as early as 1933) is visible on the right. This scene, recorded on 2 June 1956, has since been radically transformed: the station buildings and signalbox have been removed, and the track simplified with the lifting of the goods yard and the junction with the Bishops Waltham branch; a bus shelter nowadays provides limited protection for passengers using the now unstaffed halt, although electrification has resulted in a more frequent passenger service. *Anthony Burges*

Right: The Fareham–Gosport branch line began life as the first railway to reach the Portsmouth conurbation, but in its final days it was little more than a forgotten backwater. On 6 June 1953, the last day of passenger service, 'M7' No 30054 approaches Fort Brockhurst with an auto-train from Fareham. By its later years passengers had long deserted the few remaining passenger trains in favour of the frequent bus service between the two towns provided by the aged double-deckers of the Gosport & Fareham Omnibus Co (Provincial). *Anthony Burges*

FAREHAM–GOSPORT BRANCH

Centre right: Although the LSWR reached Gosport in 1848 the intermediate station of Fort Brockhurst was a later addition, in 1865. Its name referred to contemporary fortifications designed to protect the Portsmouth naval garrison. Fort Brockhurst was also the junction for the almost forgotten light railway to Lee-on-the-Solent, which operated between 1894 and 1931 (passengers) or 1935 (goods). The branch platform was situated behind the nameboard. Beyond the level crossing the line to Fareham followed a straight course for 3½ miles. *Anthony Burges*

Below: The triangle formed by the last remnant of the Gosport–Stokes Bay line was used to turn the locomotive assigned to the daily Fareham–Gosport goods. 'U'-class Mogul No 31804 treads carefully before returning to Fareham on a particularly gloomy winter's day in February 1957. *Anthony Burges*

Left: It seems that all trains on the last day of Gosport passenger service carried a commemorative headboard. 'M7' No 30054 was a frequent performer on Hampshire branch lines; here, on 6 June 1953, it is seen leaving Gosport for Fareham with 'empty stock' which, on this occasion, carries passengers. Note in the background the junction with the erstwhile Stokes Bay line. *Anthony Burges*

Below: 'M7' No 30054 takes water outside the one-road shed at Gosport whilst '700'-class 'Black Motor' No 30325 shunts in and around the semi-ruinous station, again on the last day of passenger traffic. *Anthony Burges*

Left: Notwithstanding the historic significance of the Gosport line, the end of passenger services attracted virtually no interest. A group of railwaymen exchange nostalgic memories before the departure of specially cleaned 'Q' No 30546 with the official last train to Fareham. *Anthony Burges*

Right: The colonnades of the mouldering but impressive station at Gosport, designed by Sir William Tite, whose work is also represented by Winchester and Southampton Terminus stations as well as the London terminus of the L&SR at Nine Elms. Gosport station was accorded the status of a Grade II Listed building, although the general air of dilapidation in 1953 hardly suggested that it was possible to board a passenger train within; indeed, its appearance suggested that it might be a candidate for the list of Hampshire's most haunted stations. *Anthony Burges*

Above: Evidence of bomb damage lingered at Gosport station until the end, with passenger and parcels traffic under one roof (or, more accurately, the skeleton of one roof). Its last significant royal connection was in 1901, when the body of Queen Victoria lay briefly in the royal waiting room at nearby Clarence Yard while *en route* from Osborne House, on the Isle of Wight, to the state funeral in London. *Anthony Burges*

Right: The mesh in the perimeter fence of the naval facilities at Stokes Bay was wide enough to permit this distant view of the former station, which had closed in 1915, on 23 February 1957. A favourite embarkation point of Queen Victoria on her journeys to Osborne House on the Isle of Wight, the survival of the pierhead station was quite extraordinary. *Anthony Burges*

Left: A comprehensive revision of services linking Portsmouth & Southsea with Southampton and Salisbury and Andover Junction with Romsey and Eastleigh took the form of a basic hourly frequency on each route, employing a mix of old and new steam power. Drummond 'Greyhounds' were prominent, much to the joy of contemporary railway photographers; here 'T9' No 30732 prepares to leave Portsmouth & Southsea with an all-stations service to Andover Junction on 2 November 1957. Regular-interval services were a long tradition on the Southern, and this last flourish of steam traction preceded the introduction in the late 1950s of diesel-electric multiple-units, which in turn would give way to electrification (and rationalisation). *Anthony Burges*

PORTSMOUTH & SOUTHSEA–SOUTHAMPTON

Left: 'T9' No 30732 was a regular on the Andover service, on which a fairly undemanding schedule and lightweight three-coach trains of Bulleid stock presented few challenges. Pausing at Cosham on 30 November 1957 on the final stage of its cross-country journey, the train is observed by a coal merchant unloading wagons in the adjacent yard (now the station car park). *Anthony Burges*

Left: Another 'T9', this time No 30117 (which would later achieve fame as the last survivor of its class) with an Andover train, enhances an autumnal sunset at Portchester on 30 November 1957. *Anthony Burges*

Right: Brighton 'Atlantic' survivor No 32424 *Beachy Head* attracted much attention on its daily round trip with the Brighton–Bournemouth through train. Here, on 30 November 1957, the return working has paused at Fareham before continuing to Havant and Brighton. The station at Fareham may have lost its connections to Alton and Gosport but is busier today as a result of the urban growth that occurred in the later years of the 20th century. *Anthony Burges*

Above: Swanwick was the most rural station between Portsmouth and Southampton and was the loading point for large consignments of locally grown strawberries. A reliable workhorse, '700'-class 'Black Motor' No 30306, built by Dubs & Co in 1897, had another six years of work ahead of it when photographed in March 1956. A duty such as this goods turn destined for Fareham was typical work for this class in Hampshire. *Anthony Burges*

Right: 'U'-class No 31610 makes a smart getaway from Swanwick with a Salisbury–Portsmouth train on 17 March 1956. *Anthony Burges*

Above: Also on 17 March 1956 a Portsmouth–Cardiff train hauled by a Class 4 2-6-0 rumbles across the tidal estuary of the Hamble at Bursledon with a mix of GWR, SR and BR passenger stock. *Anthony Burges*

Left: 'N'-class 2-6-0 No 31808 leads a solid consist of LSWR stock into the somewhat spartan Hamble Halt, where passenger business is brisk, with a Southampton–Portsmouth stopping train on 17 March 1956. *Anthony Burges*

Below: With their well-known propensity for poor adhesion and hesitant starts, Bulleid Pacifics were not ideally suited for duties such as this Southampton–Portsmouth all-stations working. Nonetheless, 'West Country' No 34040 *Crewkerne*, resplendent in green livery after overhaul at Eastleigh Works, makes a fine sight as it leaves Netley, again on 17 March 1956. *Anthony Burges*

Above: Sholing station was briefly under threat of closure in the 1960s. Many trains, such as this Cardiff–Portsmouth express hauled by Standard Class 4 2-6-0 No 76010 and seen on 17 March 1956, did not stop there. *Anthony Burges*

Right: Woolston goods yard is a hive of activity as 'U'-class 2-6-0 No 31623 calls at the station with a Salisbury–Portsmouth train on 12 June 1957. *Anthony Burges*

Right: Drummond 'Greyhounds' were by no means restricted to Portsmouth–Andover Junction services. On 12 June 1957 No 30729 arrives at the Southampton suburban station of Bitterne with a stopping train for Portsmouth. *Anthony Burges*

Left: Standard Class 3 2-6-2T No 82015 at Nursling on 12 January 1957 with a Southampton Terminus–Andover Junction train which is an interesting combination of old and new. *Anthony Burges*

REDBRIDGE–ANDOVER JUNCTION

Left: In 1957 Nursling retained its rural nature, although the urban encroachment of an expanding Southampton was visible to the south. Traces of the former Redbridge & Andover Canal remained to the left of the station, which opened on 19 November 1883. Passenger traffic was minimal, and few trains stopped there, so it came as no great surprise when plans were announced for its closure, which took place on 16 September 1957. To the north of the station wagonload traffic occupied the sidings opposite the signalbox. *Anthony Burges*

Below: 'T9' No 30117 leaves Romsey on 12 October 1957 with an empty hourly train for Andover Junction. *Anthony Burges*

Right: The diesel revolution in Hampshire has begun as an hourly-interval train from Salisbury to Portsmouth, formed by 'Hampshire' DEMU set No 1111, leaves Romsey on 12 October 1957. There were several occasions when failure due to teething problems resulted in the rescue of a DEMU by a Drummond 'T9' — an event known as 'Dugald's revenge'. *Anthony Burges*

Above: The sidings south of Kimbridge Junction had, in earlier days, served as a holding facility for withdrawn steam locomotives awaiting scrapping at Eastleigh. 'M7' 0-4-4T No 30379 raises the echoes as it passes the former graveyard with regulator wide open on a Portsmouth–Andover Junction train on 1 November 1957. *Anthony Burges*

Right: Standard Class 4 2-6-0 No 76013 approaches Kimbridge Junction on 1 November 1957 with an Andover Junction–Portsmouth & Southsea train. The line to the left is the important cross-country link to Salisbury. *Anthony Burges*

Left: Mottisfont station, nestling in the Test Valley some distance from the village it served, was particularly charming; note the tile-hung stationmaster's house and adjoining booking office. Oil lamps added to the period flavour, although by 1957, when this photograph was taken, the platform buildings were showing signs of age. The occasional wagonload of coal was still delivered to the small yard to the north of the station. *Anthony Burges*

Above: The variety of motive power, the dearth of passengers and the frequency of service may have been a bonus for the photographer but most certainly contributed to the red ink on the balance sheet. 'U'-class No 31803 (rebuilt at Brighton in 1928 from a 'River' 2-6-4T dating from 1926) takes its turn on an Andover Junction–Portsmouth & Southsea duty at Mottisfont on 12 October 1957. This locomotive was destined to remain in service until 1966. *Anthony Burges*

Left: A different style of station architecture prevailed at Horsebridge, but oil lamps reigned supreme. This view, captured on 12 May 1956, is in the direction of Mottisfont. Horsebridge station has today found a new role in serving the hospitality industry. *Anthony Burges*

Right: 'M7s' were regular performers on the 'Sprat & Winkle' line. On 12 October 1957 No 30356 pauses at Horsebridge with a down train. Water levels on these 0-4-4Ts must have been quite low at the end of such a lengthy trip. *Anthony Burges*

Right: Stockbridge was the principal intermediate station between Romsey and Andover and a good vantage-point for observing the most important trains — the through weekday services linking Southampton and Cheltenham Spa. Seen on 12 May 1956, this northbound train, hauled by 'U' No 31613, will work through to Cheltenham. The rolling stock is purely Great Western. *Anthony Burges*

Below: The heavier load of this southbound Cheltenham–Southampton train on 12 October 1957 required the power provided by No 7810 *Draycott Manor*, which made an impressive sight as it approached Stockbridge. By the 1950s much of the local population used Winchester as its local railhead, although in early days Stockbridge served a nearby racecourse (which closed in 1898) and until 1931 was a terminus for passengers from Whitchurch via Longparish. *Anthony Burges*

Above: South of Fullerton station the 'Sprat & Winkle' line followed the east bank of the legendary River Test. At this point passengers could catch a glimpse of fly fishermen demonstrating their skills or slaking their thirst at the Seven Stars pub. 'U'-class 2-6-0 No 31620 hurries past with an Andover Junction–Portsmouth & Southsea train on 12 May 1956. *Anthony Burges*

Left: The original station at Fullerton was known as Fullerton Bridge. With the opening of the Longparish line in 1885 it was replaced by Fullerton Junction, visible with its branch line in the background. Ironically the old Fullerton Bridge station building has outlasted the wooden structures at the junction and today, with some modifications, functions as a bed & breakfast. *Anthony Burges*

Left: The death of a country junction. A sad scene in May 1969 at Fullerton station, recorded during dismantling from the ruin of the signalbox. The route to Andover is on the left, the former Longparish branch on the right. *Anthony Burges*

Above: North of Fullerton the line followed the Anton valley towards Andover. No 7810 *Draycott Manor* was quite a frequent performer on the Cheltenham service; here the down train stops briefly at Clatford on 12 May 1956. *Anthony Burges*

Right: 'M7' No 30357 leaves Clatford *en route* to Andover with three Bulleid corridor coaches on 12 October 1957. *Anthony Burges*

Right: In spite of an hourly service and a location near the town centre, passenger business at Andover Town was relatively light. Most travellers used the junction station on the main line linking London to the West of England. The level-crossing gates were a frequent cause of traffic congestion and have been closed behind 'U'-class No 31801 and its train, bound for Portsmouth & Southsea on 12 November 1955. Population growth and the impact of associated employment when the town was designated a London-overspill site was not taken into account when the line was closed on 7 September 1964. Goods services from the Junction to the town station survived for a further three years, until 18 September 1967. *Anthony Burges*

FULLERTON–LONGPARISH

Above: Wherwell station is but a shadow of its former self in this 1953 scene looking towards Longparish. After 1913 the 15-lever signalbox, which had stood on the left, was replaced by a ground frame which controlled access to the solitary siding. The station building was a residence seldom disturbed by passing trains in a most attractive village. *Anthony Burges*

Left: It is evident that coal was the principal residual traffic on the branch in the run-up to closure in May 1956. This was the view from the brake van on 14 May 1955 as the daily goods train entered the cutting east of Wherwell. *Anthony Burges*

Left: Longparish station, built in 1884, was quite substantial and remained in good condition until the end, in spite of the fact that it had seen no passengers for more than 20 years. *Anthony Burges*

Right: Longparish yard boasted a gantry crane that formerly handled goods to and from the RAF ammunition-storage depot that functioned from 1942 until the early 1950s. On 14 May 1955 it provided an excellent vantage-point from which to observe Drummond 'Greyhound' No 30289 positioning wagonloads of coal and roof trusses. Beyond the ground frame the line extends in a south-westerly direction towards Wherwell. *Anthony Burges*

Above: Shunting in progress at Longparish on 14 May 1955. The extensive tarmac area was at one time occupied by the loading and storage facilities associated with the World War 2 RAF ammunition depot. By 1955 it was a mute reminder of events that briefly bestowed strategic significance on a 'white elephant' railway backwater. The track ended just beyond the station, after which the densely overgrown trackbed of the abandoned line to Hurstbourne extended through the Harewood Forest to the north-east. *Anthony Burges*

Right: Shunting completed, 'T9' No 30289 is ready to return from Longparish to Fullerton. Freight services were destined to survive until 28 May 1956. *Anthony Burges*

Left: Chandlers Ford station was opened in 1847 to serve the needs of a scattered farming population. By the 1950s the rapid spread of housing development from Southampton and Eastleigh was already transforming the landscape. Nevertheless, passenger services linking Eastleigh and Romsey were withdrawn on 5 May 1969, and the original station was closed. For the next 34 years the line was retained as a useful link for operating purposes while the process of suburbanisation continued. In response to the pressures created by this population growth a new station was built in 2003, served by a diesel commuter service between Romsey and Southampton via Eastleigh. The old station was interesting in that it appeared to have developed in a rather haphazard way through its 122 years of existence. All the ingredients calculated to inspire a modeller are in place in this view west towards Romsey on 31 July 1957. *Anthony Burges*

Below: A visitor to Chandlers Ford in 1957 could experience a timewarp back to the LSWR era. On 31 July 1957 'T9' No 30117, with a set of matching non-corridor coaches, continues its gentle cross-country ramble from Andover Junction to Portsmouth & Southsea. This hourly service was, paradoxically, somewhat ahead of its time as far as Chandlers Ford was concerned. *Anthony Burges*

EASTLEIGH–SALISBURY

Above: Standard Class 4 2-6-0 No 76008 leaves Dunbridge on 1 June 1957 with a Bristol Temple Meads–Portsmouth train composed of ex-GW stock. The goods yard is now history, but the station remains open as an unstaffed halt. *Anthony Burges*

Below: Standard Class 4 2-6-0s were the favoured motive power for Portsmouth–Bristol trains. On 1 June 1957 No 76065 leaves Dean, just across the Wiltshire border. A remnant of the ill-fated Salisbury & Southampton Canal, the route of which was followed quite closely by the railway between Kimbridge Junction and a point near Alderbury Junction, can be seen across the field. *Anthony Burges*

SALISBURY–WEST MOORS

Left: The countryside echoes to the deep exhaust tones of Drummond 'T9' No 30288 as it leaves Downton on 19 August 1955 with a Salisbury–Bournemouth West train. *Anthony Burges*

Right: The view south from the footbridge at Downton station on 19 August 1955. The passing-loop, signalbox and down platform saw very little use during the last years of the Salisbury–West Moors line. *Anthony Burges*

Below: Breamore was a relatively modest station where the signalbox was manned and the passing-loop was in regular use. Prominent in this northerly prospect from the down platform on 19 August 1955 is the solid LSWR stationmaster's house. *Anthony Burges*

Left: Everything about this Salisbury–Bournemouth West train at Breamore appears to be pre-Grouping in origin. Passenger services did not impose undue burdens on the 'T9' 4-4-0s in terms of either speed or load, and during the summer of 1955 veterans such as No 30288, seen on 19 August, tended to monopolise the line. *Anthony Burges*

Above: Fordingbridge, although inconveniently located for the town, was a most imposing station on the Salisbury–West Moors line. The wide forecourt reflected the needs of another age, although the goods yard handled more freight traffic than did other branch stations. Although the station has now vanished the former Station Hotel remains, albeit renamed the Augustus John Inn. At least one Fordingbridge tradition has been respected! *Anthony Burges*

Left: On 19 August 1955 'T9' No 30313 crosses the down goods at Fordingbridge with a Bournemouth West–Salisbury train composed entirely of ex-LSWR non-corridor stock. There was only one passenger on board. *Anthony Burges*

Left: Again on 19 August 1955, 'T9' No 30721 shunts at Fordingbridge prior to the arrival of an up Salisbury passenger train. *Anthony Burges*

Left: The up Salisbury passenger train having cleared the section, No 30721 is ready to leave Fordingbridge with the daily southbound goods working. *Anthony Burges*

Below: The Salisbury–West Moors line was notable for its range of station design. Daggons Road, initially named Alderholt, was a later addition opened in 1876. Brick and tiles were important outbound loads here in the early days. The station, seen here from the north, was situated across the border in Dorset and was unique on this line in possessing only one platform. *Anthony Burges*

Right: The station at Verwood was fairly modest, although its yard was usually quite busy with incoming farm supplies. *Anthony Burges*

Below: Hurdles for the construction of sheep enclosures are being unloaded at Verwood as the signalman prepares to brew the tea. Adjacent to the station in this view to the north, the Albion Hotel places Verwood firmly in the 'Strong Country'. *Anthony Burges*

Bottom: The coupling rods of 'T9' No 30304 are characteristically mellifluous as it departs Verwood with a Bournemouth West train on 19 August 1955. *Anthony Burges*

ANDOVER JUNCTION–LUDGERSHALL

Above: Signalman's view of Weyhill station, looking towards Andover Junction. *Anthony Burges*

Below: On 17 September 1955 '43xx' No 6373 pauses at Weyhill with a Swindon–Andover Junction train. *Anthony Burges*

DIDCOT, NEWBURY & SOUTHAMPTON

Right: Woodhay was the most northerly station in Hampshire on the Didcot, Newbury & Southampton line. This view north towards Enborne Lane Junction and Newbury on 19 May 1956 would be impossible to recreate, as most of this peaceful rural scene has been swallowed by the A34 trunk road. The station buildings were modest wooden structures perched on an embankment. *Anthony Burges*

Right: By the mid-1950s the Great Western flavour of the line was being diluted by the appearance of pre-Grouping vintage veterans from the Southern Railway and of BR Standard locomotive types. Here Standard Class 4 2-6-0 No 75016 disturbs the tranquillity of Highclere station on 19 May 1956 with a Southampton Terminus train. One of the delights of Highclere was a welcome cup of tea accompanied by recollections of the GWR supplied by Mr Aldridge, who was the general factotum there. Confusion arose from time to time due to the proximity of Highclere station to the village of Burghclere and the remoteness of Burghclere station from the village it purported to serve. Notwithstanding that Highclere Castle, seat of the Earls of Caernarvon, was two miles distant, the station was a fairly standard DN&S structure lacking any special goods or passenger facilities or, indeed, architectural embellishments. *Anthony Burges*

Right: Collett 0-6-0s were regular performers on the DN&S line, for which they were ideally suited. On 19 May 1956 '2251' No 2214 awaits the green flag at Burghclere before proceeding south to Southampton. Burghclere station was set in an attractive downland position, and low traffic volumes gave station staff ample time to tend the gardens and manicure the topiary work. Nearby Watership Down did not generate any shipments of rabbits from this station. *Anthony Burges*

Left: Before this section of the downs between Litchfield and Burghclere was spoiled by the incessant roar of truck traffic on the A34 the countryside could be enjoyed from a southbound train bereft of passengers. *Anthony Burges*

Left: The bucolic setting of Litchfield (Hants) station is enhanced by the arrival on 19 May 1956 of '43xx' 2-6-0 No 6313 with an empty Southampton Terminus–Newbury train. Local passengers were few and far between on the section of line between Highclere and Whitchurch Town, which was regarded by BR as something of a traffic desert. Following closure of the line in August 1964, trunk road expansion has impinged upon or obliterated parts of the former rail route in this area. *Anthony Burges*

Left: With a Newbury train receding in the distance en route for the tunnel which carried the DN&S under the former LSWR main line to the west, peace descends upon Whitchurch Town station on 20 May 1956, permitting staff to resume their gardening duties. Strategic competitive considerations had probably ruled out a connection between the lines serving Whitchurch — a decision which resulted in the construction of the Hurstbourne–Fullerton branch by the LSWR. The water tank, visible behind the up platform, dated from the 1943 capacity upgrade that transformed the DN&S into a vital strategic route for a few years. *Anthony Burges*

Right: The arrival of Drummond 'Greyhound' No 30707 on 19 May 1956 with a Newbury–Southampton Terminus train at topiary-adorned Sutton Scotney was further evidence of Southern intrusion. It was always a delight to see 'Greyhounds' in action, and in the 1950s Hampshire witnessed a last hurrah by this famous class, paralleled only by their sterling work on the so-called 'Withered Arm' in Devon and North Cornwall. *Anthony Burges*

Below: '2251' 0-6-0 No 3210 draws into the somewhat utilitarian and windswept Worthy Down Platform with a southbound train on 5 June 1957. This, the newest station on the line, was built in 1917 to serve a Royal Flying Corps depot. The station was rebuilt and a passing-loop and signalbox were added during World War 2 to handle an increase in military traffic. A short-lived feature of that period was a connecting spur to the nearby Bournemouth main line. *Anthony Burges*

Right: On its temporary return to service the legendary 4-4-0 No 3440 *City of Truro* was diagrammed to perform a leisurely weekday return trip from Didcot to Southampton Terminus. Such vintage Great Western splendour could often be enjoyed in solitary comfort on the empty trains of the DN&S, whereas today such an appearance would attract large crowds of admirers. On 5 June 1957 personnel from the nearby naval establishment have joined the southbound train, which is making a dignified exit from Worthy Down Platform and is passing the ugly World War 2 signalbox. *Anthony Burges*

Left: Kings Worthy station was opened in 1909 and by 5 June 1957 had clearly seen better days, the disused passing-loop and abandoned down platform attesting to its decline after the boom in freight traffic during World War 2. In its earlier days, local training establishments generated a significant volume of horsebox traffic, particularly to Newbury, where bloodstock could be conveyed directly to the racecourse by rail. *Anthony Burges*

Below: Again on 5 June 1957, the beautifully turned-out *City of Truro* leaves Kings Worthy for the South. In 1957 the writer made several journeys behind this vision of immaculate paintwork and shining brass as the only passenger. *Anthony Burges*

Left: By the mid-1950s the ex-Great Western station at Winchester, known variously as 'Chesil' or 'Cheesehill', seemed to be almost forgotten. Street enquiries as to its location in the city frequently elicited an assertion that it was either closed or didn't exist. Its funereal atmosphere contrasted markedly with the bustle of Winchester City station on the ex-LSWR main line. One wonders if any of the passengers awaiting the arrival of a southbound train appreciate the historical significance of the locomotive which is about to emerge from the tunnel. *Anthony Burges*

Right: City of Truro makes a fine sight leaving Winchester Chesil for Southampton Terminus on 11 May 1957 — a perfect GW assemblage. *Anthony Burges*

Right: A Sunday excursion train from Wantage Road to Portsmouth Harbour on 9 June 1957 seems to be racing a Royal Blue coach on an amazingly deserted (by today's standards) Winchester by-pass. It is sad to reflect that Wantage Road station and much of the route taken by this train, in addition to its locomotive and rake of 10 GW coaches, are now but distant memories. *Anthony Burges*

Below: No 3440 *City of Truro* joins the main line at Shawford Junction with its Didcot–Southampton Terminus train. The long brick viaduct which carried the connecting line to the DN&S proper on the eastern side of Winchester paralleled the by-pass and is visible in the background. Note too that the train is taking the diversionary route that followed the main line to Shawford & Twyford and was designed to alleviate congestion on the busy main line. The date is 1 May 1958. *Anthony Burges*

ALTON–WINCHESTER

Above: Butts Junction, situated a mile and a half west of Alton, was the point where the Mid-Hants and Meon Valley (right) lines and a truncated remnant of the Basingstoke & Alton Light Railway (left) formerly converged. On 2 November 1957 'M7' No 30481 accelerates away from Alton on the climb over the 'Alps' with an Eastleigh train. *Anthony Burges*

Left: 'M7' No 30125 propels an auto-train for Alton as it plunges into the chalk cuttings through the 'Alps' after leaving Medstead & Four Marks on 5 June 1957. *Anthony Burges*

Above: The historic value of the Mid-Hants line as a diversionary route for the Bournemouth main line was exemplified by the passing loops that existed at all intermediate stations. In later years before closure (and subsequent revival and preservation of the section between Alton and Alresford) the only loops remaining were those at Medstead & Four Marks and Alresford. Regular use of Medstead & Four Marks as a passing-place is confirmed by this view of 'M7' No 30125 pausing with an auto-train bound for Alton, again on 5 June 1957. *Anthony Burges*

Right: Immaculate topiary work, rural tranquillity and vestiges of the former up platform gave no hint of the changes that in the years ahead were destined to transform Ropley station into the location of the locoshed and workshop of the 'Watercress Line'. *Anthony Burges*

Right: Until their replacement by DEMUs Drummond 'M7' 0-4-4Ts monopolised passenger services on the Mid-Hants line, as typified by No 30125 leaving Ropley with an Alton–Eastleigh train, once again on 5 June 1957. *Anthony Burges*

Left: Alresford station slumbers on a beautiful summer's day in 1957. By now the Mid-Hants line appeared to be living on borrowed time, and soon DEMUs would herald a final chapter in the history of the line prior to its inevitable closure. Such a gloomy prospect did not take into account the railway preservation movement that was to grow and flourish throughout Britain during the latter half of the 20th century, and today the once deserted platforms are thronged with visitors. *Anthony Burges*

Below left: The LSWR ambience that prevailed at Alresford is epitomised by this meeting on 15 June 1957 of the down goods, headed by 'Black Motor' 0-6-0 No 30693, and an up auto-train *en route* to Alton propelled by 'M7' No 30480. Such a scene represented the very quintessence of the line before the advent of the DEMUs. *Anthony Burges*

Above right: The reincarnation of the Alton–Alresford section, which began in 1977, did not save the link between Alresford and Winchester Junction. Thus it was that the intermediate station of Itchen Abbas — and any possibility of reviving a diversionary route for the electrified Bournemouth main line — was lost. On the now abandoned section 'M7' No 30328 approaches Itchen Abbas with an Alton–Eastleigh train, again on 15 June 1957. *Anthony Burges*

Right: An Eastleigh train pauses amidst rural surroundings at Itchen Abbas on 15 June 1957. *Anthony Burges*

Right: Station architecture at Itchen Abbas resembled that at Ropley and Alresford. A mantle of ivy did much to soften the stuccoed severity of the building. *Anthony Burges*

MEON VALLEY

Left: On 10 August 1954 '700' 0-6-0 No 30308 pauses at the diminutive platform at Farringdon with the 7.38am train from Alton to Fareham. In the final years this was the only passenger working on the Meon Valley line that was not operated by a Drummond 'M7' tank and, due to its early departure from Alton, was seldom photographed. *Anthony Burges*

Left: An unusual feature at Farringdon was the massive and unlovely corrugated-iron goods shed which bore the name 'Farringdon Halt', although the nearby single-coach-length platform was never accorded the designation 'halt' in the public timetable. *Anthony Burges*

Below: 'Black Motor' 0-6-0 No 30693 approaches Farringdon with an Alton–Farringdon goods in February 1957. The station would serve as the area's freight railhead for a further 13 years after the cessation of passenger services, complete closure being effected on 13 August 1968. *Anthony Burges*

Right: On 5 February 1955 'M7' No 30054, a regular performer on the branch during the final years, awaits delivery of the token at Tisted while working the 07.58 Fareham–Alton train. Sombre overcast skies, intermittent drizzle and characteristically chilly February temperatures seemed appropriate for this, the final day of passenger service. *Anthony Burges*

Below: The impressive if somewhat isolated station at Tisted, replete with ample siding accommodation, presented a convincing LSWR image, the exception being the inevitable pre-cast-concrete Southern Railway ganger's hut. Beyond the solitary van remaining in the yard the line curves away northwards to Farringdon. Such a scene seemed to invite the attention of the railway modeller. The station is now a private dwelling and is surrounded by recent housing development. *Anthony Burges*

Above: Privett station stood 519ft above sea level, the summit of the line. In later years only one platform was in regular use, and the ground frame in the former signalbox was normally switched out. The railway cottages are visible to the north of the station, whilst to the left, through the trees, stood Ye Olde Privett Bush (now known as the Pig and Whistle), where the landlord liked to regale visiting railway enthusiasts with tales of ghost trains. The station building still exists as a (very) private residence, well screened from the inquisitive by several decades of planting and tree growth. *Anthony Burges*

Left: Again on 5 February 1955, the last day of passenger service, 'M7' No 30054 draws into the grassy platforms at Privett with an Alton train. Passenger traffic at Privett was always light, as the village it served was a mile and a half distant. *Anthony Burges*

Below left: Privett, in common with other stations on the branch, had something of the air of an Edwardian country house. The 'pagoda-style' gents was a typical feature. *Anthony Burges*

Above right: The north portal of Privett Tunnel after the track had been lifted in August 1958. Indicative of the massive engineering and earthworks which characterised this short-lived branch line, the bore, which cut through the downland, was 1,056yd in length. Following the closure the tunnel was used for several years for mushroom cultivation. *Anthony Burges*

Right: Apart from the tunnels at Privett and West Meon, the most impressive engineering work on the line was undoubtedly West Meon Viaduct. It was dismantled in 1956. *Anthony Burges*

Left: Once again on the last day of passenger service, 5 February 1955, 'M7' No 30054 propels the 9.5am Alton–Fareham auto-train at West Meon. The station clearly had not received a coat of paint for many years. This contrasted with the common practice of the time, when the repainting of rural stations was often a reliable indicator of impending closure. *Anthony Burges*

Right: Situated in a deep cutting, the platforms at West Meon were designed with 10-coach Waterloo–Gosport trains in mind, although for the most part such main-line pretensions remained just a dream. After the wooden footbridge at the north end was removed the break in the platforms at the south end provided access. Such an economy measure, also implemented at Wickham and Tisted, was perhaps an early recognition that the line was destined never to rise above the status of obscure rural backwater. *Anthony Burges*

Left: On the last day of regular service the 11.56 Fareham–Alton train, augmented to four coaches, takes water at West Meon. The heavier-than-usual train was the reason for this rare occurrence, which gave some of the enthusiast passengers on board an unexpected photographic opportunity. *Anthony Burges*

Right: Built to main-line standards to handle traffic that never materialised, the Meon Valley line was one of the worst investments ever made by the LSWR. Siding capacity at West Meon was generous, and in this view the railway cottages north of the station are adjacent to a water tank that may have supplied the water column on the up platform. *Anthony Burges*

Right: '700' 0-6-0 No 30326 approaches Droxford with a down goods. The unusually heavy load of nine wagons plus brake van suggests that the train was clearing the yards between Farringdon and Droxford on the last day. *Anthony Burges*

Below: A relatively busy moment at Droxford on 10 August 1954 as 'M7' No 30054, on a Fareham–Alton passenger service, passes 'T9' No 30726 on a southbound freight. Short trains, long platforms and the absence of footbridges presented the few passengers with excellent walking opportunities. The nameboards at Droxford made the dubious claim 'Droxford for Hambledon'. Given that the latter, the birthplace of cricket, was 3½ miles distant it is perhaps not surprising that there is no record of crowds of cricket historians besieging the station. *Anthony Burges*

Above: '700' No 30326, with the last goods train from Alton, waits to cross a northbound passenger service at Droxford as a cluster of enthusiasts and locals await a last ride north. There was sufficient goods traffic handled at Droxford to justify the continuance of freight service from Fareham for a further seven years. In 1970 Droxford was the scene of the short-lived railcoach experiment which was conceived as the salvation of the Isle of Wight railways. *Anthony Burges*

Left: 'M7' No 30055 approaches Droxford with a Fareham–Alton train strengthened to four coaches on the last day of passenger service. By a strange coincidence consecutively numbered 'M7s' — Nos 30054 and 30055 — provided power for most Meon Valley trains on this sad occasion. *Anthony Burges*

Left: Mislingford siding survived until 30 April 1962, when the Fareham–Droxford goods service was withdrawn. In addition to incoming farm supplies an important customer at Mislingford was the Meon Valley Timber Company. Contrasting with the situation at Farringdon, no halt was ever provided here, as the local population was very sparse. *Anthony Burges*

Right: By the time 'T9' No 30726 reached Wickham with the Alton–Fareham goods on 10 August 1954 its load had been reduced to just a brake van. Although Wickham was the largest community located on the Meon Valley line its station conformed to the standard design in every respect. Bus competition had already captured most of the passenger traffic here. *Anthony Burges*

Right: The unstaffed halt at Knowle served a large mental hospital. In the mid-1950s the few trains that stopped here were mainly Meon Valley services. The two tracks closest to the camera carried Fareham–Eastleigh trains which avoided the Knowle tunnels, the latter being the route taken by the branch trains. Local soil instability subsequently resulted in the diversion of DEMUs on the Fareham–Eastleigh route to the single-track section as far as Knowle, although the halt had by then been obscured by vegetation. *Anthony Burges*

Below: 'M7' No 30054 pauses at Knowle Halt with the 13.30 Alton–Fareham train on 10 August 1954. *Anthony Burges*

BENTLEY–BORDON

Left: Two '2-BIL' units approach with a Waterloo–Alton service whilst 'M7' 0-4-4T No 30027 waits at Bentley with a connecting train for Bordon in July 1957. *Anthony Burges*

Centre left: Having left Bentley, 'M7' No 30110 heads south to Bordon with the branch passenger train on 15 September 1957. The electrified line to Alton is visible in the background. *Anthony Burges*

Bottom left: The bucolic scene near Blacknest Gap is enhanced by 'M7' No 30110 as it passes with a well-filled auto-train from Bordon to Bentley on 15 September 1957, the last day of passenger service. The passenger accommodation consists of an LSWR ironclad set modified for push-pull operation. *Anthony Burges*

Above: The Bordon–Bentley auto-train powered by 'M7' No 30110 gathers speed after slowing for an ungated level crossing south of Blacknest Gap. *Anthony Burges*

Right: It was unusual for the short platform at Kingsley Halt to be thronged by so many passengers, but this was a unique occasion. It's 26 September 1953, and well-polished 'L12' 4-4-0 No 30434, the last survivor of its class, pauses for a brief photostop whilst on a railtour special visiting the Longmoor Military Railway and other delights. No 30434 would be withdrawn in 1955. *Anthony Burges*

Right: The rural location of Kingsley Halt is evident as No 30110 departs for Bordon on the last day of operation. Note the youthful fireman. *Anthony Burges*

Above: Further evidence of footplate hospitality on the Bordon branch as 'M7' No 30027 approaches Bordon with a train from Bentley in July 1957. The tracks to the right are those of the main line of the Longmoor Military Railway, which had its own platform adjacent to the branch terminus at Bordon. *Anthony Burges*

Left: The view from Bordon station in July 1957, showing the attractive building housing the ground frame and, beyond, the connection to the Longmoor Military Railway. The line to Bentley curves off to the left in the distance. *Anthony Burges*

Left: 'M7' No 30027 and the branch train are dwarfed by the platform at Bordon, which was designed to handle troop trains. *Anthony Burges*

Above: Longmoor Military Railway No 401 *Major General McMullen*, converted to oil-firing in the 1950s, was a 2-8-0 'Austerity' type built by the Vulcan Foundry in 1945. Traditionally it had been used for VIP duties, and here it is about to leave Bordon LMR station on 26 September 1953 with an enthusiasts' special for Longmoor Downs. The train included two ex-Southern Railway invalid saloons, designated 'officers only'; among other hand-me-downs from the SR was a three-coach ex-SECR 'birdcage' set, reserved for 'other ranks', which was noted for its imaginative if lurid internal graffiti. *Anthony Burges*

LONGMOOR MILITARY RAILWAY

Right: Seen approaching Bordon with a freight from Longmoor on 26 September 1953 is LMR 'Austerity' 0-6-0 saddle tank No 178. Built by Robert Stephenson & Hawthorn in 1945, it was to end its days at Woodham's scrapyard at Barry in 1963. *Anthony Burges*

Right: Another LMR 'Austerity' 0-6-0 saddle tank, No 181 *Insein*, built at Vulcan Foundry in 1945, approaches Longmoor with a train from Liss on the same day. *Anthony Burges*

Left: Stroudley 'Terrier' 0-6-0T No 32661 approaches Havant with a train from Hayling Island in abnormal winter conditions during January 1965. The first coach is the experimental plastic-bodied BR Standard non-corridor No S1000, which is now preserved on the East Somerset Railway at Cranmore. *G. R. Siviour*

HAVANT–HAYLING ISLAND

Left: The Hayling Island branch may have been only 4½ miles in length, but on summer Saturdays it was served by express trains. In July 1958 a Southdown bus and a line of traffic wait for Stroudley 'Terrier' No 32650 to negotiate the level crossing at Langston with a non-stop Hayling Island–Havant train. This working was an exception to the normal practice whereby returning trains ran bunker-first. *Anthony Burges*

Below: A most evocative sunset scene on 2 November 1965, in which one of the last trains to run on the Hayling Island branch crosses Langston Bridge. Note that the railway spelled 'Langston' without an 'e' on the end. *G. R. Siviour*

Right: After the 1,100ft-long timber bridge with opening span across the Langstone Channel, the first station on the island was North Hayling. Seen here in July 1958, this simple wooden structure was in a remote location bordered by salt marsh and heathland. The gentleman on the platform is an onlooker rather than a traveller; few of the latter used North Hayling. The diminutive size of 'Terrier' No 32661 is emphasised by the BR Standard Mk 1 non-corridor coach which almost obscures the view from the footplate. *Anthony Burges*

Below: The neat terminus at Hayling Island served the populated southern end of the island, from which the line drew its commuters and which was a destination for holidaymakers. A small quantity of goods traffic was still handled in the 1950s. *Anthony Burges*

Right: Platform capacity at South Hayling limited trains to three coaches. On this occasion (July 1958) No 32661 has a mix of pre-Grouping, Southern and British Railways rolling stock for the short run to the mainland to make connection with the electrified Waterloo–Portsmouth Harbour and Brighton–Portsmouth Harbour routes at Havant. The weak timber viaduct at Langstone Harbour, which had restricted branch motive power to the 'A1X' tank engines, was also cited by BR as justification for closure, effected on 2 November 1963. The loss of this charming and well-patronised branch line was widely regretted. *Anthony Burges*

BOTLEY–BISHOPS WALTHAM

Left: 'M7' No 30375 pauses for the photographer at the site of Durley Halt with a Bishops Waltham–Eastleigh goods on 12 January 1957. The halt had closed to passengers on 2 January 1933. *Anthony Burges*

Below left: The view towards Botley at Bishops Waltham station on 12 January 1957. The station canopy would be removed ahead of final closure. *Anthony Burges*

Top right: No 30375 has just arrived at Bishops Waltham with the daily goods train on 12 January 1957. Parcels traffic is being dealt with by the station staff. *Anthony Burges*

Above: Shunting in progress at Bishops Waltham on 12 January 1957. Note the water tower and the attractive goods shed. Bishops Waltham would survive as a freight railhead until 30 April 1962. *Anthony Burges*

Right: A rare moment at Bishops Waltham was the arrival of a 'C14'-class 'Potato Can' 0-4-0T on an enthusiasts' special from Eastleigh on 14 June 1952. Here No 30589 is about to replenish its limited water capacity before the return trip. The aroma of hot oil permeated the coaches as we 'raced' across the fields to Eastleigh at 25mph. *Anthony Burges*

READING–REDHILL

Above: Tucked away at the north-east extremity of the county,
Blackwater station was provided with a slow and somewhat infrequent
cross-country service, typified here by Standard Class 4 2-6-0
No 76056 on a Reading South–Redhill train on 23 August 1955.
This scene has now been transformed, and the goods yard is history,
but Blackwater survives as an unstaffed halt with an improved
passenger service compared with that of 50 years ago. *Anthony Burges*

Railway Magazines from

Ian Allan
PUBLISHING

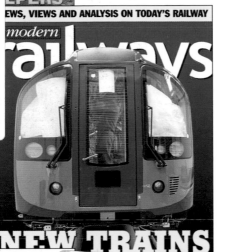

Railways Illustrated
Monthly £3.50
Offers the highest quality editorial and photographic coverage of the UK railway scene, with a particular focus on news and topical events.

Modern Railways
Monthly £3.60
The voice of the UK rail industry; with in-depth and informed comment, the latest news on British and European railways, recruitment pages and analysis of industry trends.

Locomotives Illustrated
Quarterly £3.50
Each issue is entirely devoted to detailed coverage of a particular distinguished class of locomotive.

Steam Days
Monthly £3.60
Highlights from the days when steam power reigned supreme.

www.ianallanpublishing.com

ISBN 0-7110-3164-9

9 780711 031647

Printed in England

£12.99

Ian Allan
PUBLISHING